Rats Rule!

'Rats Rule!'
An original concept by Elizabeth Dale
© Elizabeth Dale 2022

Illustrated by Guadalupe Andrade

Published by MAVERICK ARTS PUBLISHING LTD
Studio 11, City Business Centre, 6 Brighton Road,
Horsham, West Sussex, RH13 5BB
© Maverick Arts Publishing Limited August 2022
+44 (0)1403 256941

A CIP catalogue record for this book is available at the British Library.

ISBN 978-1-84886-902-8

www.maverickbooks.co.uk

This book is rated as: Turquoise Band (Guided Reading)

Rats Rule!

By **Elizabeth Dale**

Illustrated by **Guadalupe Andrade**

Leo was so excited as his mum dropped him off at school. It was Pet Day and today was the first time he'd ever had a pet to take and show. And Rishi was the best pet ever!

Leo felt so proud as he carried Rishi's travel cage into the playground.

"Hey, Leo! What's in there?" asked Amir. Other children crowded round.

"Yeah, let's see!" cried Sally. And then, she screamed.

"Shhh!" said Leo, backing away. "You'll frighten Rishi!"

"But I saw a long tail!" gasped Sally.

"It's... it's a rat!"

"Yuck!" said Amir. "Rats are gross!"

"He isn't gross!" Leo retorted. "Rats are brilliant and really intelligent. Rats rule!"

"Oh yeah?" laughed Amir.

"Yeah," said Leo. "For example, he can…"

But his words were drowned out by the bell and everyone hurried inside.

Sally rushed into the classroom ahead of Leo. "Watch out! Leo's got a nasty, vicious, smelly rat!" she cried.

Some children shrieked, so Leo quickly opened the cage door and reached in to stroke poor, frightened Rishi.

"Children, sit down and stop making such a fuss," said their teacher, Mrs Biggs. "We're lucky that Leo has brought his lovely rat in to show us. He isn't nasty or smelly at all."

"But rats live in sewers!" yelled Mo.

"Not Rishi," said Leo. "He's not wild.

He's got a lovely, clean cage."

"Yes," said Mrs Biggs. "Just like your hamster, Mo. Now, everyone put your cages at the back, and let's start our lessons."

But Leo couldn't concentrate on his work. He'd thought that his class would love Rishi, not hate him. They didn't even know anything about him!

Finally, it was breaktime. It was Leo's class's turn for the climbing frame. Everyone was too busy playing to make any more nasty comments about rats.

As soon as break finished, Leo rushed inside to check on Rishi. He stared in horror. No! Rishi's cage door was wide open and there was no sign of him anywhere.

"Rishi's gone!" he cried.

Everyone started shrieking, sitting on desks and standing on chairs. Mrs Biggs quickly told them to calm down.

"I can't understand how it happened," she said, rushing over to help Leo search. "Nobody's come in, I've been in here all break."

Leo turned to her, horrified. "Oh no," he said, "then it must be my fault. I stroked Rishi earlier. I can't have shut the cage door properly."

"I'm sure we'll find him," said Mrs Biggs. "Put up your hand if you'd like to help search, and the rest of you please quietly continue with your maths work."

Everyone chose to help look. They peered under chairs and cushions, behind books and lunch boxes. But Rishi was nowhere to be found.

"I think we should all sit back down quietly," said Mrs Biggs. "Maybe then we'll hear Rishi rustling or scratching somewhere? Leo, you can sit by his cage in case he returns."

Leo sat there, feeling miserable. He should never have brought Rishi to school. Today was a disaster!

Time ticked by and there was no sign of Rishi. Leo was starting to think he'd never see Rishi again. But just then, he saw a little pink nose peeking through a narrow gap between the floorboards. It was Rishi!

Quickly, Leo grabbed a piece of carrot from his cage and held it out.

"Come here, Rishi. Come on, boy," he whispered. And slowly, Rishi did just that! Leo gasped when he saw Rishi had something silver in his mouth.

It was a necklace! Leo gently picked Rishi up and took it from him.

"Look!" he cried. "Rishi's back. He was under the floorboards and look what he found down there!"

Mrs Biggs rushed over. "Oh!" she cried. "That's the silver locket my granny gave me. It fell off my neck weeks ago. I thought I'd lost it forever. Oh, Rishi! Thank you! How clever of you to squeeze through that tiny gap and find it."

Leo smiled proudly as he put Rishi back inside his cage.

"Right, class, time for assembly," Mrs Biggs said. "I'll ask the headmaster if we can show Rishi to the rest of the school. After how clever Rishi has been, it would be good to explain just how great pet rats are!"

The headmaster agreed to include Rishi in the assembly.

Leo stood on the stage and told everyone about how wonderful Rishi was. About how he kept himself cleaner than any other pet, even cats. How he was a fantastic swimmer and climber, and extremely clever. So clever, that he'd sniffed out Mrs Biggs's lost necklace.

When he'd finished, everyone clapped and Leo smiled proudly. And then, from the back, Amir yelled, "Rishi's great. Rats rule!" Leo laughed and, as everyone cheered, it seemed the whole school agreed.

Quiz

1. Why did Leo bring Rishi into school?
a) It was his birthday
b) It was Pet Day
c) He wanted to do a show and tell

2. What is Leo's teacher called?
a) Mrs Jones
b) Mrs Briggs
c) Mrs Biggs

3. How did Rishi escape?
a) He squeezed through the bars
b) He chewed a hole in the bars
c) Through the open cage door

4. What did Leo use to tempt Rishi out from between the floorboards?
a) Chocolate
b) A piece of apple
c) A piece of carrot

5. What missing item did Rishi find?
a) A locket
b) An earring
c) Money

Turn over for answers

Book Bands for Guided Reading

The Institute of Education book banding system is a scale of colours that reflects the various levels of reading difficulty. The bands are assigned by taking into account the content, the language style, the layout and phonics. Word, phrase and sentence level work is also taken into consideration.

Maverick Early Readers are a bright, attractive range of books covering the pink to white bands. All of these books have been book banded for guided reading to the industry standard and edited by a leading educational consultant.

To view the whole Maverick Readers scheme, visit our website at www.maverickearlyreaders.com

Or scan the QR code above to view our scheme instantly!

Quiz Answers: 1b, 2c, 3c, 4c, 5a